MW01659601

Hi there,

Did you know studies have shown that saying "bad" words makes shit feel a little better? That's just fucking science! So, if today's got you feeling pissy, try letting it out with some profane penmanship practice. Worried you'll screw up? Did you notice my handwriting isn't perfect? First of all, fuck you. Second, it's fine. Perfection is never the aim. Have fun with it and just practice. That's the goal!

Enjoy!

♡Heather

Welcome to the shitshow.

Welcome to the shitshow.

nope. nope. nope.

Zero fucks left

Zero fucks left

Shut your damn mouth.

Shut your damn mouth.

This is fine.

This is fine.

Don't be a dick.

Don't be a dick.

Happy fucking birthday

Happy fucking birthday

Boss ass bitch

Boss ass bitch

Certified bad ass

Certified bad ass

Fancy as fuck

Fancy as fuck

It's about damn time.

It's about damn time.

This shit is bananas.

This shit is bananas.

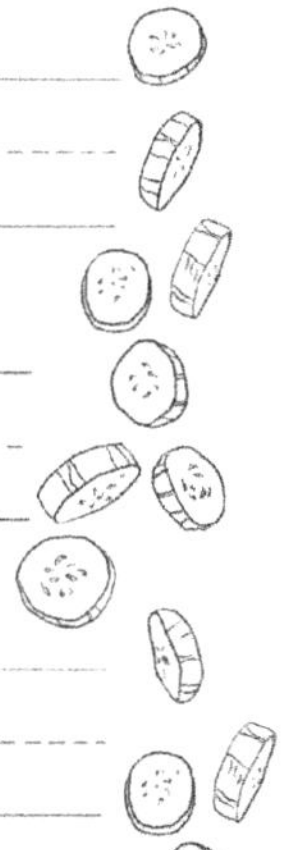

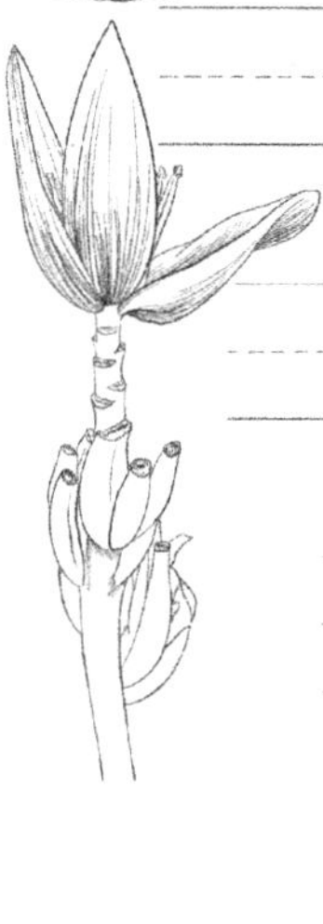

My favorite color is petty.

My favorite color is petty.

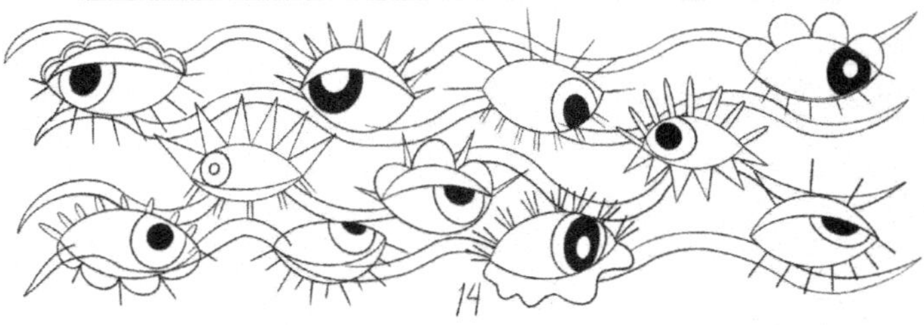

Guys, chill the fuck out.

Guys, chill the fuck out.

Get shit done.

Get shit done.

You're such a douche canoe.

You're such a douche canoe.

I'm going back to bed.

I'm going back to bed.

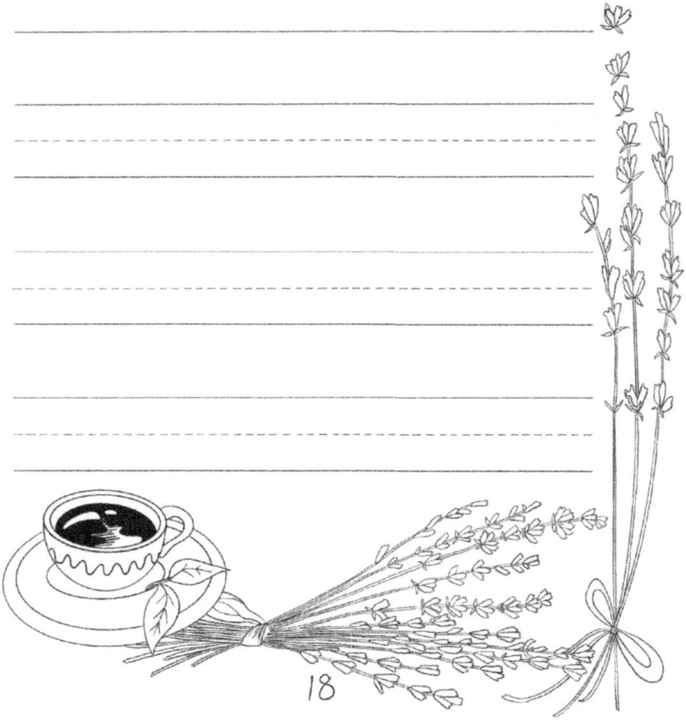

Every damn day

Every damn day

Fuck this shit.

Fuck this shit.

I'm not for everyone.

I'm not for everyone.

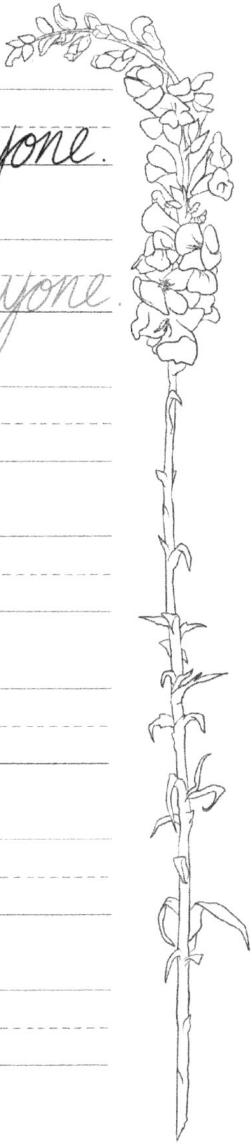

That's some bullshit.

That's some bullshit.

Not today, Satan.

Not today, Satan.

Mind your own damn business.

Mind your own damn business.

Wanna bitch about bitches?

Wanna bitch about bitches?

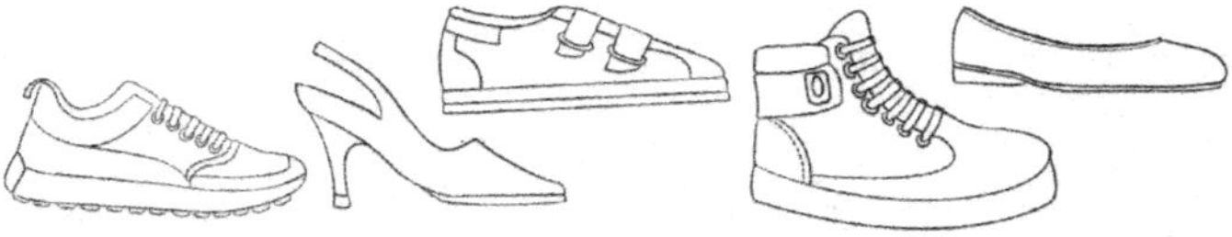

Kickass! Kickass!

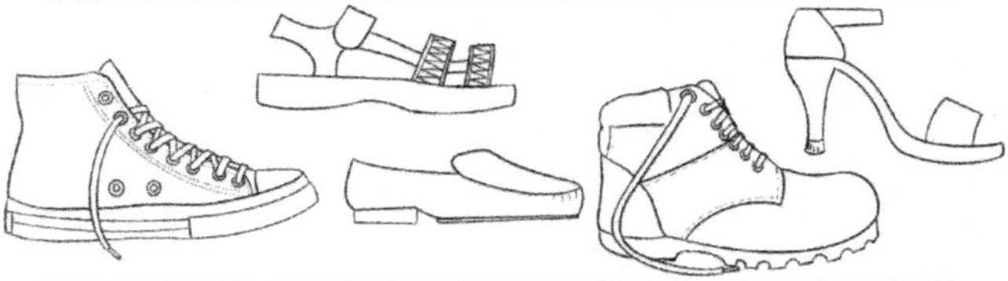

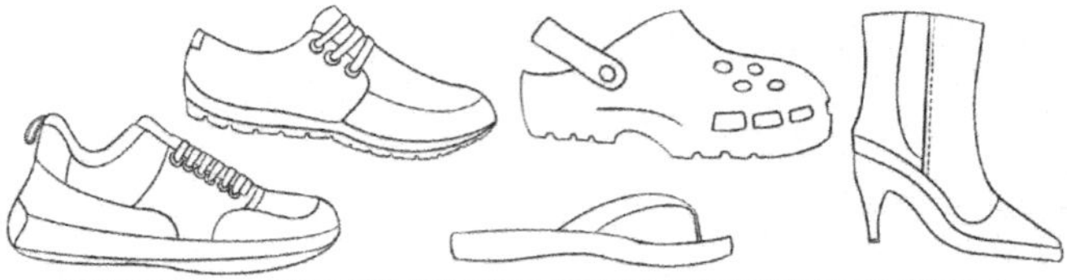

That's a terrible idea. I'm in.

That's a terrible idea. I'm in.

I don't know a damn thing.

I don't know a damn thing.

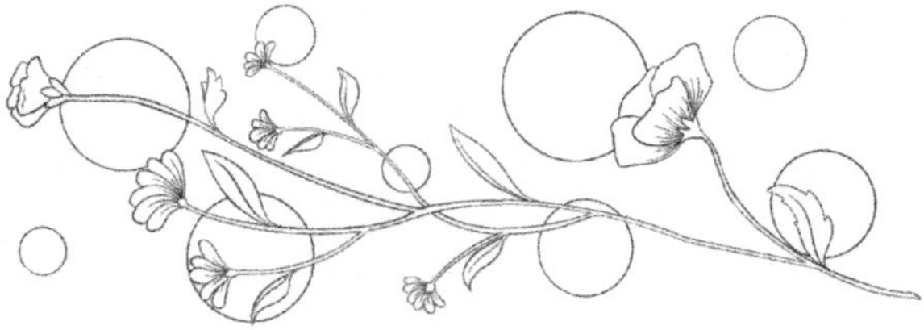

I'd rather be at home.

I'd rather be at home.

Keep practicing! Write your own tiny curses here.

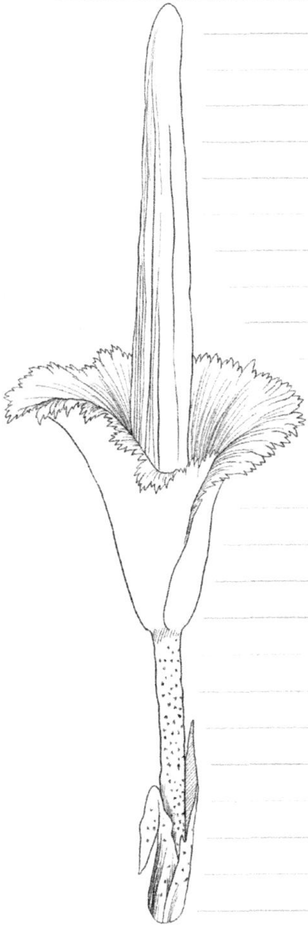

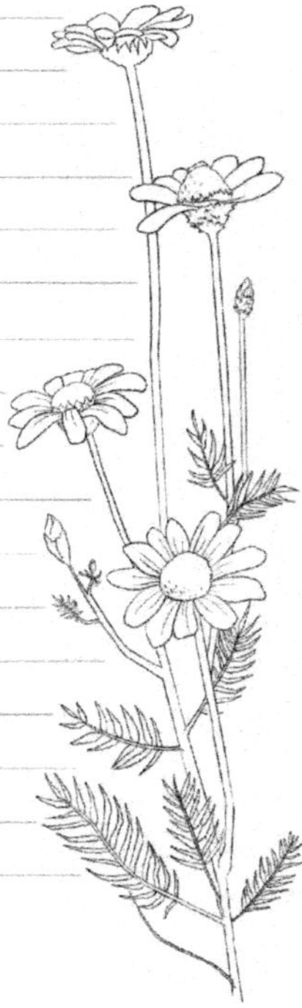

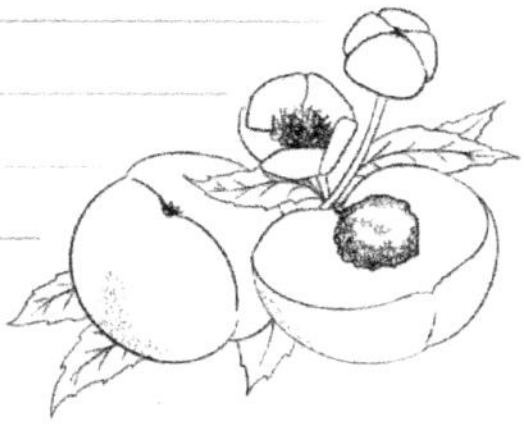

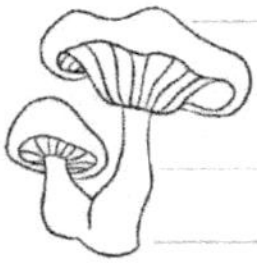

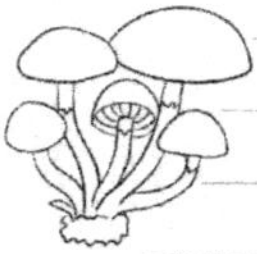

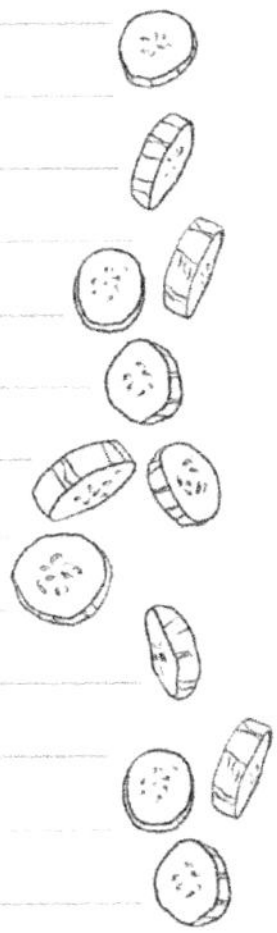

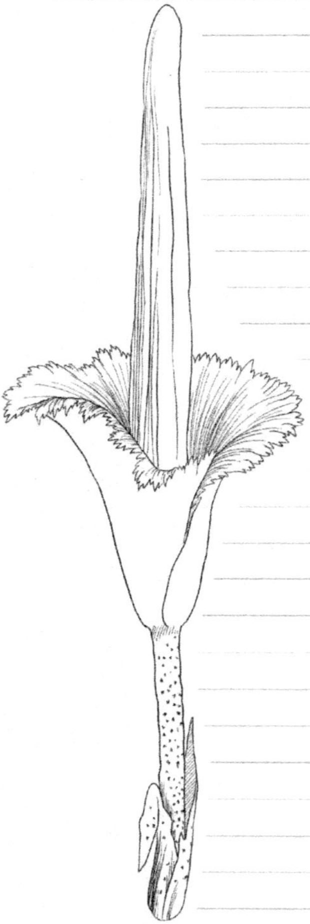

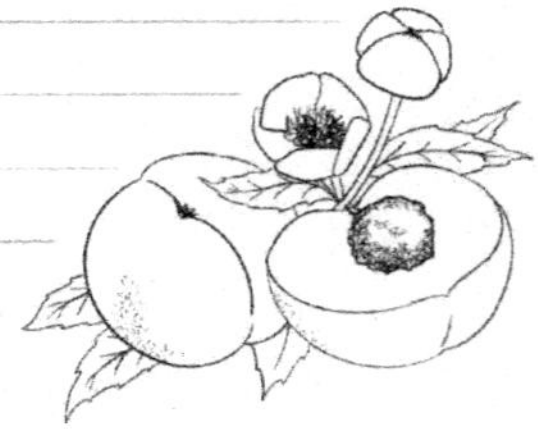

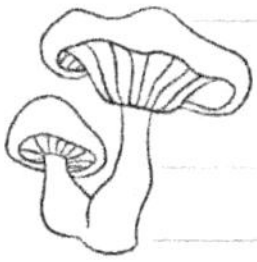

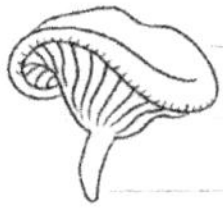

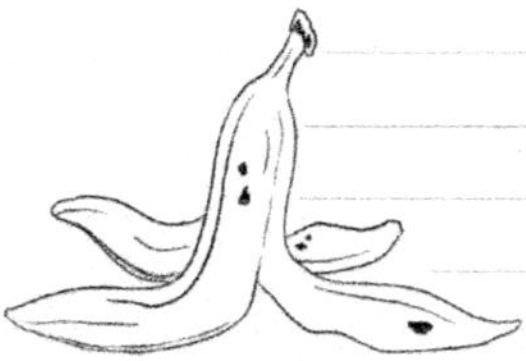

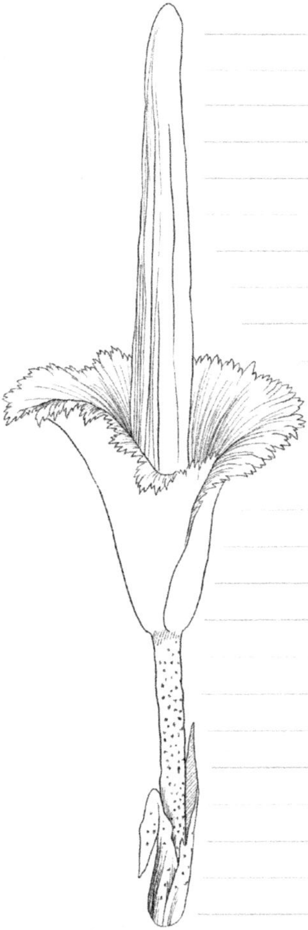

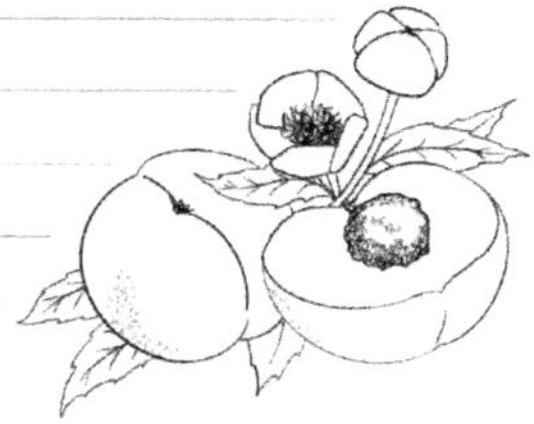

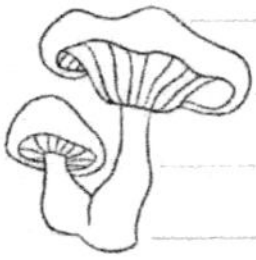

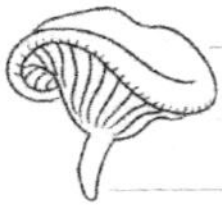

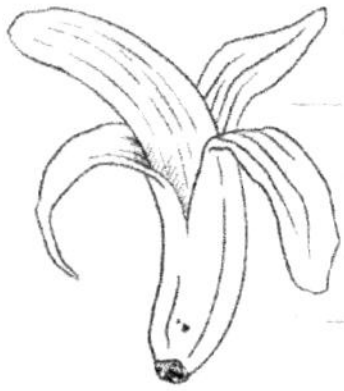

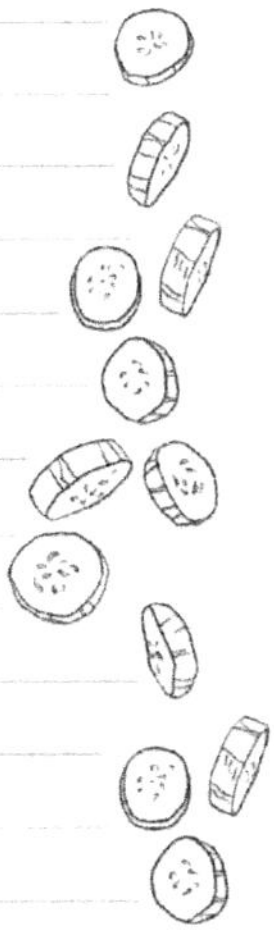

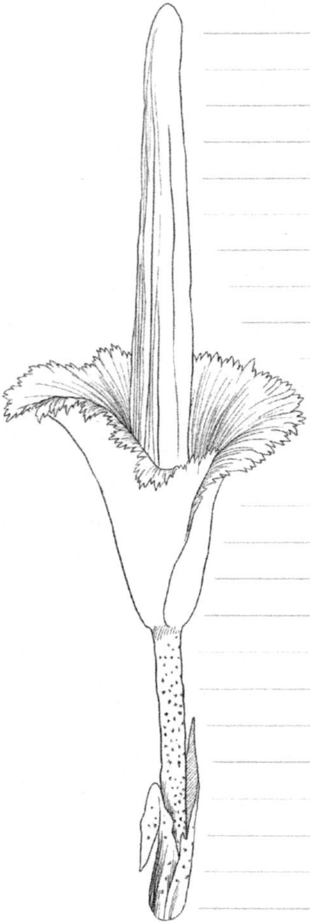

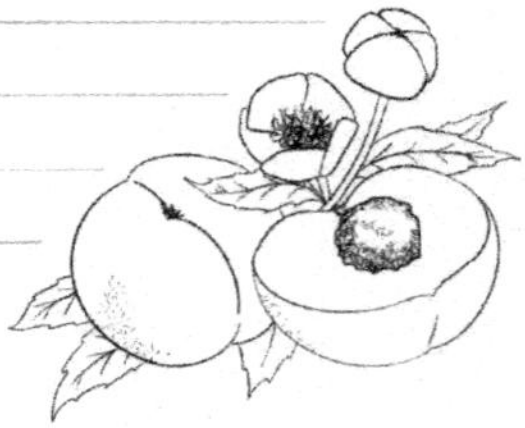

Made in the USA
Coppell, TX
10 September 2023

21427555R00036